TONE AND TECHNIQUE

THROUGH CHORALES AND ETUDES

BY JAMES D. PLOYHAR AND GEORGE B. ZEPP

**AN IDEAL COMBINATION
FOR THE IMPROVEMENT OF TECHNICAL FA[...]
ARTICULATION, INTONATION AND TO[...]**

FOREWORD

This unusual book brings to music educators and students of today some of the time-honored studies by Arban, Klose, Concone, Shantl, Pares and Saint-Jacome. They are presented in an interesting format with twenty-four of the most popular chorales from traditional literature.

THE CHORALES

To insure a rich, full band sound all chorales are scored in four basic parts (A-B-C-D). They may also be performed very effectively by any small ensemble in which all four parts are represented. Some of the more obvious of many possible instrumental combinations are:

BRASS QUARTET: 1st Trumpet (A) 2nd Trumpet (B) 1st Trombone or Horn
        (C) 2nd Trombone or Horn (D)
CLARINET QUARTET: 1st Clarinet (A) 2nd Clarinet (B) Alto Clarinet (C) Bass Clarinet (D)
SAXOPHONE QUARTET: 1st Alto (A) 2nd Alto (B) Tenor (C) Baritone (D)

THE ETUDES

These excellent studies can be played in unison by the entire band or band class. The director may then assign the etude to any section or combination of instruments, while the remainder of the group plays the BAND PART. Like the chorales, these accompaniments are scored in four basic parts (A-B-C-D). Harmonically and rhythmically complete, they transform the useful "exercise" into an enjoyable musical experience.

THE DUETS

Written by acknowledged masters of instrumental pedagogy, the six duets add yet another dimension to musical growth and development. The band is divided into two balanced sections in any manner the director may choose. The two parts are written to provide equal challenge for all players. Repetition without monotony may be achieved by exchanging parts for a second playing.

SPECIALIZED SCALE AND TECHNICAL STUDIES

The final section consists of etudes composed for particular families of instruments by specialists in each category. The SIX SCALE STUDIES for woodwind instruments are by Pares, with brass accompaniments by James D. Ployhar. The EIGHT TECHNICAL STUDIES, written for brass instruments by Arban and Saint-Jacome, have woodwind accompaniment. All of these etudes offer valuable and challenging technical workouts designed to meet specific needs.

INSTRUMENTATION AND PART ASSIGNMENT

Conductor
Flute (A-8va higher)
Eb Clarinet (A)
Bb Clarinet (A-B)
Eb Alto Clarinet (C)

Bb Bass Clarinet (D)
Oboe (A)
Bassoon (D)
Eb Alto Saxophone (A-B)
Bb Tenor Saxophone (C)

Eb Baritone Saxophone (D)
Bb Trumpet/Cornet (A-B)
Horn in F (C)
Horn in Eb (Mellophone) (C)
Trombone (C-D)

Baritone T.C. (D)
Baritone B.C. (D)
Bass (Tuba) (D-8va lower)
Drums (rhythm)
Bells (A)

CONTENTS

O Thou Joyful Day

Sicilian Folk Song

Four Eighth Notes in Contrast to Half Notes

Etude No. 1

Klose

Band Part

See, the Conqueror Mounts in Triumph

Dutch Traditional Melody

Staccato Eighth Notes

Etude No. 2

Klose

Moderato

Band Part

Moderato

Ye Watchers and Ye Holy Ones

German Traditional

Eighth and Sixteenth Notes

Etude No. 3 Allegretto

Klose

Band Part

Allegretto

Hymn to Joy

Ludwig van Beethoven

Eighth Notes Followed by Two Sixteenth Notes

Etude No. 4

Arban

Moderato

Band Part

Moderato

The God of Abraham Praise

Traditional Hebrew Melody

Dotted Eighths and Sixteenths

Etude No. 5

Arban

Allegretto

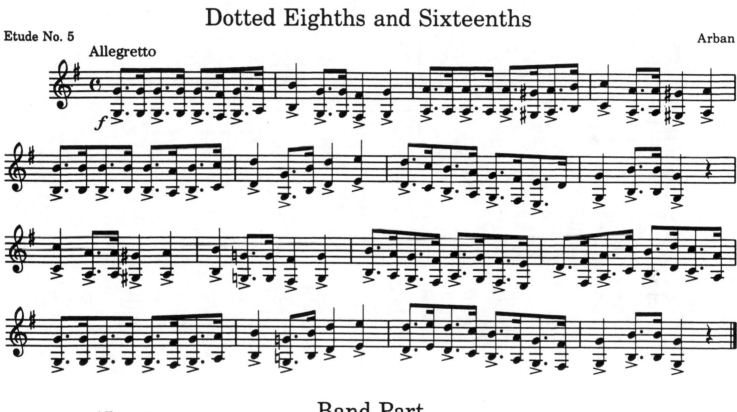

Band Part

Allegretto

8

O Word of God Incarnate

German Chorale

Dotted Eighths and Sixteenths in 3/4

Etude No. 6

Klose

Moderato

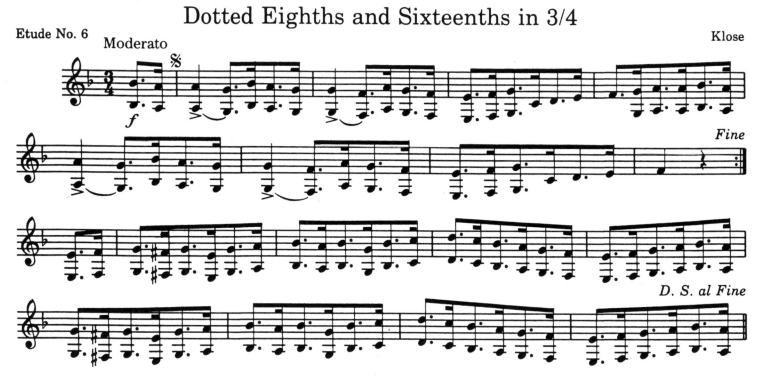

Band Part

Moderato

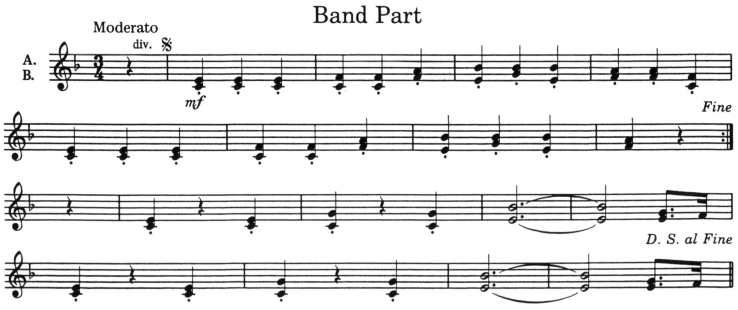

E.L. 3176

O Worship the King

Michael Haydn

Mixed Notation in Common Time

Etude No. 7   Allegro

Concone

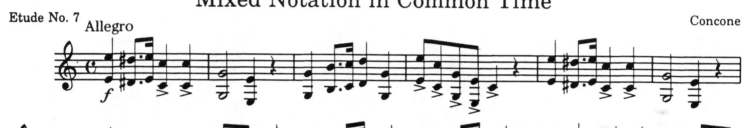

Band Part

E.L. 3176

Ein' Feste Burg

Luther

Alla Breve or Cut Time

Etude No. 8

Klose

Band Part

Sleepers, Wake

Johann Sebastian Bach

Syncopations and Ties from Bar to Bar

Etude No. 9

Klose

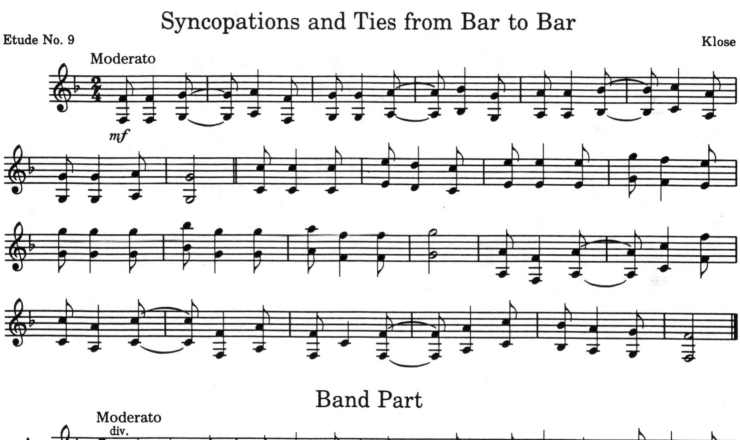

Band Part

E.L. 3176

12

Again, as Evening's Shadow Falls

Jeremiah Clark

Triplets

Etude No. 10

Maestoso

Band Part

Maestoso

E.L. 3176

With Songs and Honors Sounding Loud

Traditional German Melody

Triplets on the First Quarter Note

Etude No. 11

Klose

Allegro moderato

Band Part

Allegro moderato

Come, Children, Join to Sing

Spanish Melody

Study in 3/8 Time

Etude No. 12

Band Part

Good Men, Rejoice

German Medieval Melody

Slow 6/8 Time

Etude No. 13   Andante (In 6)   Arban

Band Part

Andante (In 6)

E.L. 3176

Integer Vitae

Friedrich F. Fleming

Fast 6/8 Time

Etude No. 14

Allegro moderato (In 2)

Band Part

Allegro moderato (In 2)

Come, My Soul, Thou Must Be Waking

Franz Josef Haydn

Variation on a Famous Melody

Etude No. 15

Arban

Moderato

Band Part

Moderato

E.L. 3176

Austrian Chorale

Franz Josef Haydn

Study in 9/8 Time

Etude No. 16

Band Part

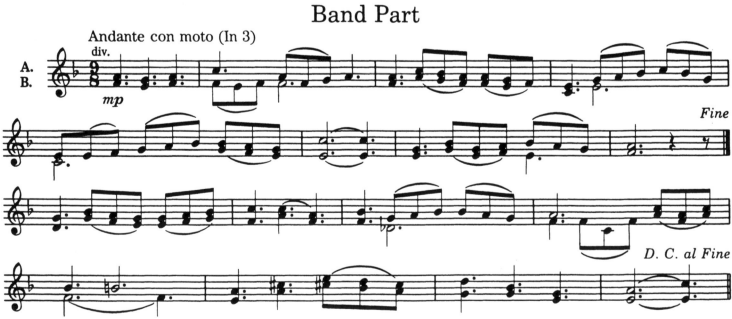

E.L. 3176

Now Thank We All Our God

Johann Cruger

Mixed Notation in 9/8 Time

Etude No. 17

Schantl

Andante (In 3)

Band Part

Andante (In 3)

E.L. 3176

Lo, How a Rose

16th Century Melody

Study in 12/8 Time

Etude No. 18

Andante moderato (In 4)

Arban

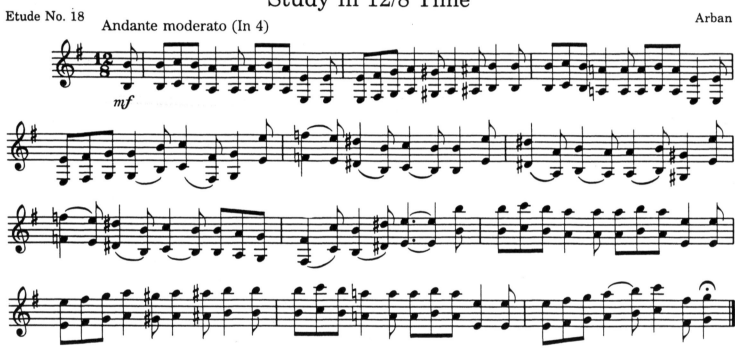

Band Part

Andante moderato (In 4)

Vesper Chorale

Ascribed to
D. Bortnyanski

Duet in Alla Breve or Cut Time

Etude No. 19

Saint-Jacome

Duet Part

E.L. 3176

Greenland

Michael Haydn

Duet in Fast 6/8 Time

Etude No. 20

Tollot

Allegro moderato (In 2)

Duet Part

Allegro moderato (In 2)

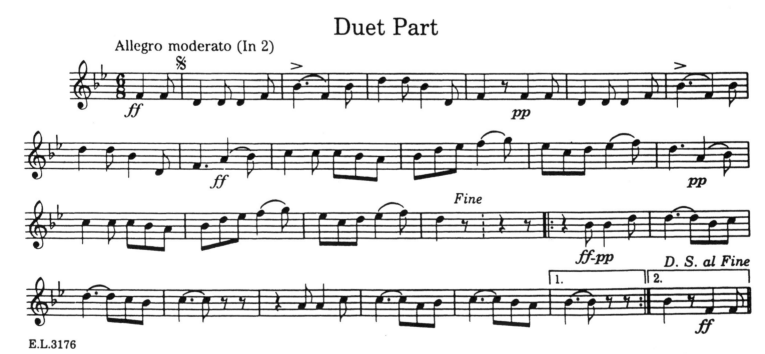

Greensleeves

Old English Melody

Staccato Eighth Notes and Syncopation

Etude No. 21

Saint-Jacome

Duet Part

E.L. 3176

Father, Blessing Every Seedtime

Sir Arthur S. Sullivan

Mixed Notation in 2/4

Etude No. 22

Saint-Jacome

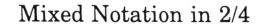

Duet Part

E.L. 3176

Break Forth, O Beauteous Heavenly Light

Johann Sebastian Bach

Mixed Notation in Alla Breve or Cut Time

Etude No. 23

Saint-Jacome

Duet Part

E.L. 3176

Creation

Franz Josef Haydn

Duet in Slow 6/8 Time

Etude No. 24

Saint-Jacome

Andante (In 6)

Duet Part

Andante (In 6)

E.L. 3176

Scale Study in B♭ (Concert)
(Woodwinds Only)

Etude No. 25   Pares

Scale Study in E♭ (Concert)
(Woodwinds Only)

Etude No. 26   Pares

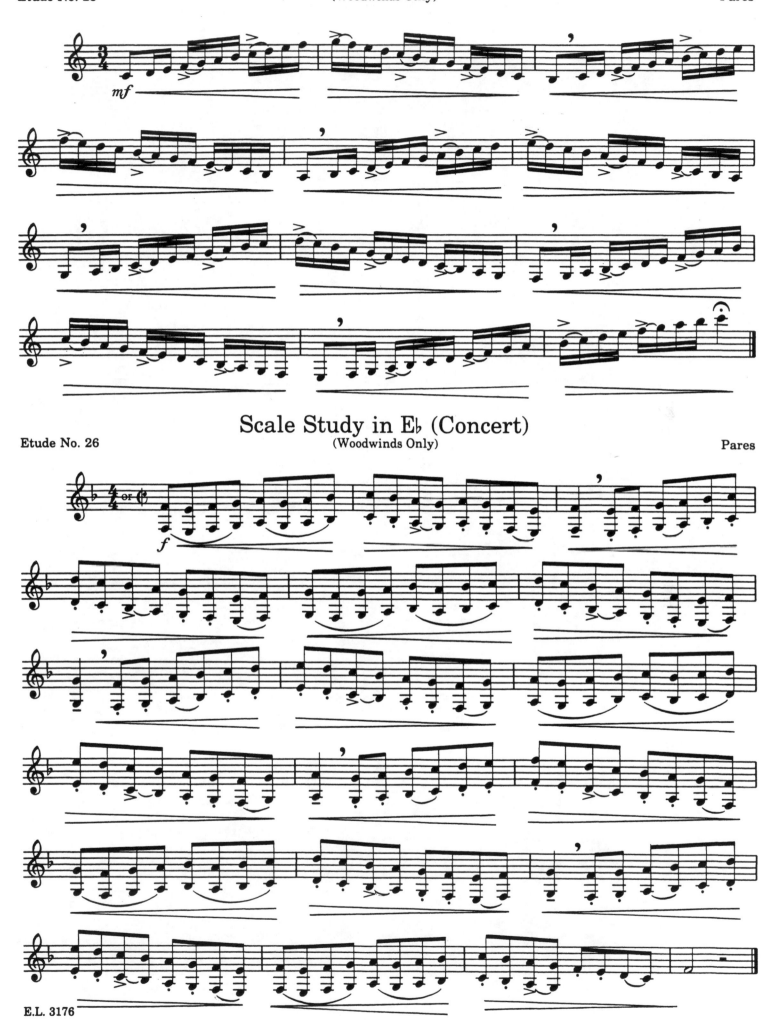

Scale Study in C (Concert)
(Woodwinds Only)

Pares

Scale Study in F (Concert)
(Woodwinds Only)

Etude No. 28

Pares

Scale Study in D♭ (Concert)
(Woodwinds Only)

Etude No. 29   Pares

Scale Study in A♭ (Concert)
(Woodwinds Only)

Etude No. 30   Pares

Velocity Study with Eighth Notes
(Brasses Only)

Etude No. 31
(Band Accompaniment)

Arban

Work for speed!

Velocity Study with Triplets
(Brasses Only)

Etude No. 32
(Band Accompaniment)

Saint-Jacome

Work for speed!

E.L. 3176

Interval Study
(Brasses Only)

Saint-Jacome

Etude No. 33
(Band Accompaniment)

Velocity Study with Sixteenth Notes
(Brasses Only)

Etude No. 34
(Band Accompaniment)

Saint-Jacome

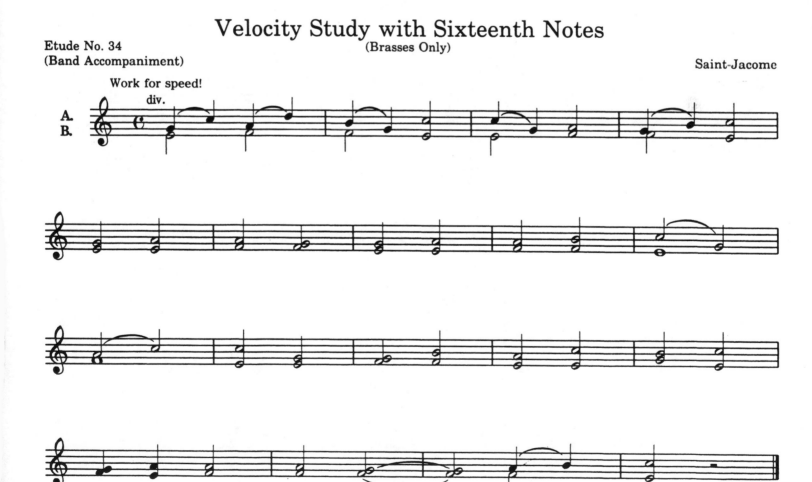

Double Tonguing
(Brasses Only)

Etude No. 35
(Band Accompaniment)

Arban

Double Tonguing
(Brasses Only)

Etude No. 36
(Band Accompaniment)

Arban

Triple Tonguing
(Brasses Only)

Etude No. 37
(Band Accompaniment)

Arban

Triple Tonguing
(Brasses Only)

Etude No. 38
(Band Accompaniment)

Saint-Jacome

E.L. 3176